Yeah I'm tired!!

A 7 day quick devotional for nurses

By
Jennifer Dewberry Taylor,
BSN, RN

DEDICATION

This devotional is dedicated to my parents. The two people who showed me how to be a giver, true servant, and to love unconditionally. With so much love, I thank you, both

INTRODUCTION

Tired physically, mentally, emotionally.... Just flat-out tired! Sometimes, you just want to SCREAM!!! Your boss is getting on your nerves, or maybe you are the boss, and your team is getting on your nerves. Dare we mention the patient and their families. That's a whole different ball game, and that's just work, not your personal life!

But it's all okay, right? Remember who you are. Better yet, remember Whose you are! Yep! Your Father is the Almighty. The One who wraps us in His loving arms and comforts us when we are in those low places. You know! The places where we are tired and are close to throwing in the towel. Yes, that place! Let's dive into His word a bit and find some quick comfort!!!

Day 1

Because of the extravagance of those revelations, and so I wouldn't get a big head, I was given the gift of a handicap to keep me in constant touch with my limitations. Satan's angel did his best to get me down; what he did was push me to my knees. No danger then of walking around high and mighty! At first, I didn't think of it as a gift, and begged God to remove it. Three times I did that, and then he told me,

My grace is enough; it's all you need.

My strength comes into its own in your weakness.

Once I heard that, I was glad to let it happen. I quit focusing on the handicap and appreciated the gift. It was a case of Christ's strength moving in on my weakness. Now I take limitations in stride, and with good cheer, these limitations that cut me down to size—abuse, accidents, opposition, bad breaks. I just let Christ take over! And so the weaker I get, the stronger I become.

2 Cor 12:7-10 MSG

So, let's break this down. Today you may be feeling weak. Weak in your walk with God, weak at work, weak at home, or just feeling low or down. But just because you are feeling weak does not mean you have to stay that way. Think about it! When caring for a patient in a healthcare setting or in the home, we recognize that we are there for a reason. We help the patients get through whatever they need to get through. Rehab, post-op, transitioning from this life, etc. We are their strength at that moment. This is what God is to us, right? Think about the supportive devices used. They are usually made of some metal… strong and sturdy, able to hold a patient's weight! That is what God is to us! When the patient regains strength, what happens? We leave or they leave. The device is picked up by the DME company or is stored in a closet. Is this what we do to God after giving us His strength to get through our weakness? Are you allowing God to be your continual support, or just when you think you need Him most? He is there. He is always there. Tuck Him deep in your heart. Not just a closet where He is not seen. Tuck Him deep in your soul so you may always feel His presence!

Take a quick moment and allow this prayer to lead you into your intimate time with God.

Heavenly Father, Thank you! Thank you for allowing me to see and feel Your presence and strength. Thank you for coming into my life and living within me. Please continue to remind me of your presence. Continue to remind me I am never alone, even when I am at a low point! Remind me that Your Strength is a Gift, especially for me at this moment! Help me to move past this with courage, strength, and joy! Amen.

Take a moment to write down your thoughts and prayers

_____

_____

_____

_____

_____

_____

_____

_____

_____

_____

_____

_____

_____

_____

_____

_____

_____

_____

_____

_____

_____

_____

_____

Take a moment to write down your thoughts and prayers

_____

_____

_____

_____

_____

_____

_____

_____

_____

_____

_____

_____

_____

_____

_____

_____

_____

_____

_____

_____

_____

_____

_____

_____

_____

_____

_____

_____

Day 2

Hear my cry, O God; Listen to my prayer. From the end of the earth I call to You, when my heart is overwhelmed and weak; Lead me to the rock that is higher than I [a rock too high to reach without Your help]. For You have been a shelter and a refuge for me, A strong tower against the enemy. Let me dwell in Your tent forever; Let me take refuge in the shelter of Your wings. Selah.

Psalms 61 1-4 AMP

Having an overwhelming moment, day, or days? In this passage, we know that David had those feeling, too. We are human. It is written all throughout the Book of Psalms about David's feelings. So, who are we that we should not experience some as well? It is not necessarily what we feel but what we do with what we feel. Here David is praying, asking God for help. He is reminding not only himself but also reminding God He has been that Rock, Shelter and Refuge. David is overwhelmed. Overwhelmed with life. Have you felt that feeling of being overwhelmed or even anxious? It's hard to be a nurse and never have this feeling, even if it is for a moment. No matter how often you feel these feelings or how long they last, we know that God is here for us. We know that he is never too far away and is our refuge.

Take a moment and relax. Take a deep breath; in….and out…in…and out. Fix your mind on Jesus. Imagine Him wrapping His warm and protective arms (wings, as David calls them) around you. Imagine those arms being so comforting and loving. Allow your muscles to relax as He lifts and protects you. While in His presence, release those feelings that are not like Him. Allow him to take on those feelings. He is our Strong Tower. Trust me, He can handle it!

Now use this time to tell Him how you feel! Just talk/pray to Him. He is there listening and waiting just for you!

Take a moment to write down your thoughts and prayers

_____

_____

_____

_____

_____

_____

_____

_____

_____

_____

_____

_____

_____

_____

_____

_____

_____

_____

_____

_____

_____

_____

Take a moment to write down your thoughts and prayers

_____
_____
_____
_____
_____
_____
_____
_____
_____
_____
_____
_____
_____
_____
_____
_____
_____
_____
_____
_____
_____
_____
_____
_____
_____

Day 3

Then Jesus said, "Come to me, all of you who are weary and carry heavy burdens, and I will give you rest. Take my yoke upon you. Let me teach you, because I am humble and gentle at heart, and you will find rest for your souls. For my yoke is easy to bear, and the burden I give you is light."

Matt 11:28-30 NLT

Often, we get tired mentally, physically, emotionally, and spiritually. We feel burned out. Burned out at work, home, in church or just in life. Here, Jesus is telling us He wants us to come with Him! Look at what he is offering us, REST, COMFORT, PEACE. You know those things you get when your problems are weighing you down and you cannot take any more of anything? These problems could be sin, or maybe being mistreated or wronged. Or this problem could just be your exhaustion in your search for God. He is allowing us to live freely with JOY. This is an opportunity for REST. We should always seek this as a nurse, nurturer and givers of self. What do you consider the best treatment for self-care? We all know self-care is important for functioning in our best capacity. Why not go to the Source of self-care?

Matthew 7: 7-8 talks about how prayer can be effective. In these two verses, Jesus tells us to ask, seek, and knock so it can be given, found, and opened. Verse 8 (NLT) tells us what happens if we simply follow instructions. *"For everyone who asks, receives. Everyone who seeks, finds. And to everyone who knocks, the door will be opened"*.

What do you need from God right now at this moment? What do you desire that could give you rest?

Take this time and center yourself. Allow your mind to focus solely on those things you ask of God, the things you need, and His presence. Allow your breathing to calm and your muscles to relax. Speak to Him, knowing He is listening. Pour your heart out. It's just you and God. Your Savior. Your Creator. Your Best Friend. Speak openly and freely.

Don't know where to start? Include this prayer: Sweet Father! I come to you heavy and in need of more of You. Please allow me to feel Your comfort so I may have rest. I want more of You. I need more of You. Help me recognize that You are always there, and I can call out for help from You. Help increase my faith in You, knowing you hear me, and you will give me the comfort, peace, safety, and rest that comes with Your Grace. In Your Name, I claim it and believe it! Amen.

Take a moment to write down your thoughts and prayers

_____

_____

_____

_____

_____

_____

_____

_____

_____

_____

_____

_____

_____

_____

_____

_____

_____

_____

_____

_____

_____

_____

Take a moment to write down your thoughts and prayers

_____
_____
_____
_____
_____
_____
_____
_____
_____
_____
_____
_____
_____
_____
_____
_____
_____
_____
_____
_____
_____
_____
_____

Day 4

Then David arose from the earth, and washed, and
anointed himself, and changed his apparel, and came
into the house of the LORD, and worshipped: then he
came to his own house; and when he required, they set
bread before him, and he did eat.

2 Sam 12:20

In this scripture, David came out of a period where he fasted and wept because his child had fallen ill and died. This chapter talks about how David sinned against the Lord. What is important is that David recognized what he needed to do. He washed his face, got himself together, and worshipped the Lord.

Sometimes, we may unknowingly fall short or allow our ways, feelings, and thoughts to get in front of those of God. Doing this can bring on things we are totally not expecting. Think about it! How often have we done something that will make us look good in the eyes of others or make us feel good? Like taking a position that will give us more money and give us authority out of season (Eccl 3:1). After doing these things, different emotions can be attached to the attention we have attracted. Kind of like the things we have talked and prayed about over the past couple of days. We know that anxiety, fear, overwhelming feelings, etc., are not of God. Like, more duties, encountering disgruntled staff, etc. We know that he may have allowed it, but he did not send that to us. But we unknowingly opened the door for those things to creep into our circle and spirit when our focus shifts from being on God and what he has for us to ourselves and what is pleasing to us or, as some would call it, our flesh. This is called carnality or having a carnal mind or thoughts. Once we ask him to take this away, we cannot allow it to come back just because it is pretty to our eyes.

Now is the time to do as King David did. Wash our faces, get ourselves together, worship our Lord, and walk in our God-given destiny. We recognize where we need to change. Let's do it!

Take a moment to think about the things you may need to change. The things that can help you grow in your walk with God and the things that can attract others to God through you. Allow your thoughts to center and focus on God. Remember, He is right there listening to you. Tell Him how you feel and ask Him to continue to help you to grow in His will!

Take a moment to write down your thoughts and prayers

_____

_____

_____

_____

_____

_____

_____

_____

_____

_____

_____

_____

_____

_____

_____

_____

_____

_____

_____

_____

_____

_____

_____

_____

_____

Take a moment to write down your thoughts and prayers

_____
_____
_____
_____
_____
_____
_____
_____
_____
_____
_____
_____
_____
_____
_____
_____
_____
_____
_____
_____
_____
_____
_____
_____
_____
_____

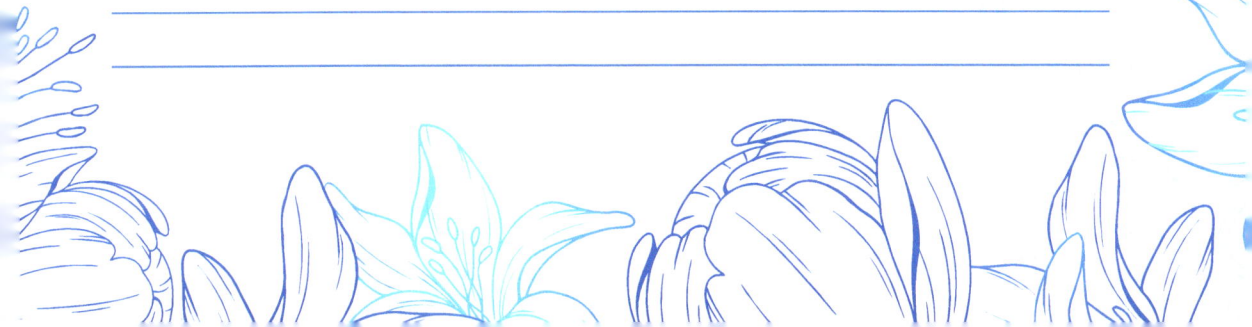

Day 5

Do not fear [anything], for I am with you;
Do not be afraid, for I am your God. I will strengthen
you, be assured I will help you;
I will take hold of you with My righteous right hand
[a hand of justice, of power, of victory, of salvation].

Isaiah 41:10 AMP

In the scriptures, before this, it is referencing Israel, God's chosen people. Isaiah is foretelling how God's people (this will be all believers) will be brought out of captivity. Are there times you have felt like you were in captivity with the world's weight crushing you? Yeah, I think we all have experienced that a time or two. Whether it lasts for an extended period or just a moment, it is a feeling that can be unshakable. One thing we can hold deeply in our hearts is that God is with us. How often does the Bible mention the Right Hand? Think of its significance. Do words like strength, power, honor, blessings, and protection come to mind? If all of that is right beside God, at His Right Hand (take a deep breath), what does that mean for us? How does that make him view us as believers? How does that make you feel?? Excited, thankful, blessed, overwhelmed with love, maybe?? Going through the hard times feels horrible. But always remember He has promised us that trouble will not last always (1 Peter 5:10).

Take another deep breath and center yourself. As you take more deep breaths, place your thoughts on God. Place your hand over your heart and feel your heartbeat. Feel this knowing that God makes that happen. Next, place your hand over your stomach. Feel yourself take deep breaths in and out. Feel this knowing that God does that. Now talk to Him. Do not be afraid. He is right there with you.

Take a moment to write down your thoughts and prayers

_____

_____

_____

_____

_____

_____

_____

_____

_____

_____

_____

_____

_____

_____

_____

_____

_____

_____

_____

_____

_____

_____

_____

Take a moment to write down your thoughts and prayers

_____

_____

_____

_____

_____

_____

_____

_____

_____

_____

_____

_____

_____

_____

_____

_____

_____

_____

_____

_____

_____

_____

_____

_____

_____

Day 6

But they that wait upon the Lord shall renew their
strength; they shall mount up with wings as eagles; they
shall run, and not be weary, and they shall walk, and
not faint.

Isiah 40:31KJV

Did you know there is strength in patiently waiting on God? Waiting on God will provide you with the time to focus on Him. In your waiting, talk to Him and listen to what He says. Just calling His name will renew your strength. Remember, there is power in the name of Jesus (1John 5:13-15). While you are waiting, expect something. These expectations will help us on our journey in our Christian walk through life. What should you expect? For starters, your strength. Think of the eagle. An eagle's wingspan can be 5ft or more, giving them the strength (there's that word again!) to soar high above the earth. Think about their vision. God gives an eagle the vision to see things that our naked eyes can't see from that distance. He uses an eagle to show us how much strength he can give us. We are his greatest accomplishment, not the eagle. Think about that!

Put your trust in God. He will never leave you nor will He lie to you (Numbers 23:19). So focus on that. Keep it close to your heart as you patiently ride out the storms of life.

Take a moment to write down your thoughts and prayers

_____

_____

_____

_____

_____

_____

_____

_____

_____

_____

_____

_____

_____

_____

_____

_____

_____

_____

_____

_____

_____

Take a moment to write down your thoughts and prayers

_____
_____
_____
_____
_____
_____
_____
_____
_____
_____
_____
_____
_____
_____
_____
_____
_____
_____
_____
_____
_____
_____
_____

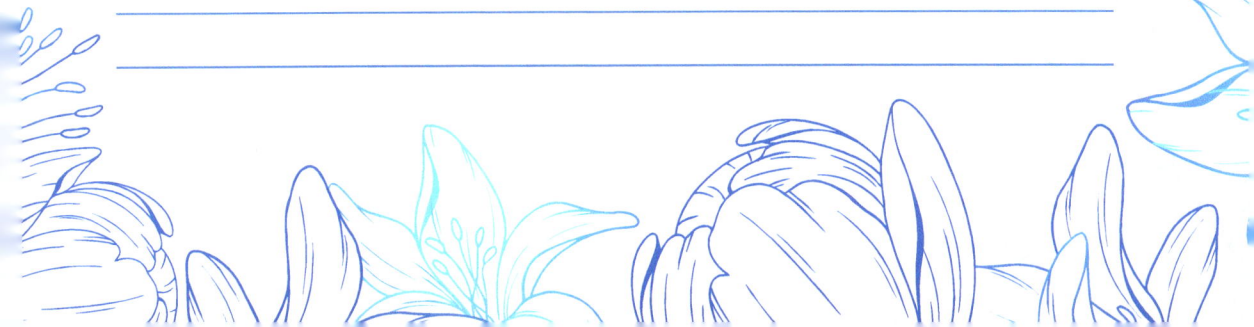

Day 7

Three things will last forever—faith, hope, and love—
and the greatest of these is love.

1 Cor 13:13NLT

God has given us great gifts. Of those great gifts, we have faith, hope, and love. Paul wrote the people of Corinth because they were struggling. Struggling with some of what we have struggled with over the last past six days. In those letters, God guided Paul to teach us how to continue our walk with Him and help grow the Kingdom.

Let's look at the gifts beginning with faith. What is faith to you? Remember that faith is us believing what we can't see (Heb 11:1). Sometimes, our faith may become weak, but it doesn't have to stay that way. Remember, His Grace is always sufficient (1 Cor 12:9).

Next is hope. Where does your hope lie? Or should I ask, in Whom does your hope lie? Hope is trusting or having confidence that what you believe will happen. You can't have hope without faith. Hold on to your hope (Heb 10:23)!

Lastly is Love: The greatest gift, right? Love has led us to be givers, nurturers, caregivers… nurses. This is what God has planted on the inside of each of us. It is up to us to use what He has given!

Let this scripture lead you into your next prayer. While reading it, focus on God. "We remember before our God and Father your work produced by faith, your labor prompted by love, and your endurance inspired by hope in our Lord Jesus Christ." 1 Thess1:3

Now talk to Him!

Here's a starter: Heavenly Father, I come before you boldly by faith, hoping your love will live on the inside of me. I am asking for it to be shown through me to glorify You. Thank you, God, for giving me the strength, peace, and confidence to continue this journey. Thank you for allowing me to grow in my destiny. Although I may feel weak at times, God, I know you are there providing me with love, patience, guidance, and strength. Thank you, Jesus! Amen.

Take a moment to write down your thoughts and prayers

_____
_____
_____
_____
_____
_____
_____
_____
_____
_____
_____
_____
_____
_____
_____
_____
_____
_____
_____
_____
_____
_____
_____

Take a moment to write down your thoughts and prayers

_____
_____
_____
_____
_____
_____
_____
_____
_____
_____
_____
_____
_____
_____
_____
_____
_____
_____
_____
_____
_____
_____
_____
_____

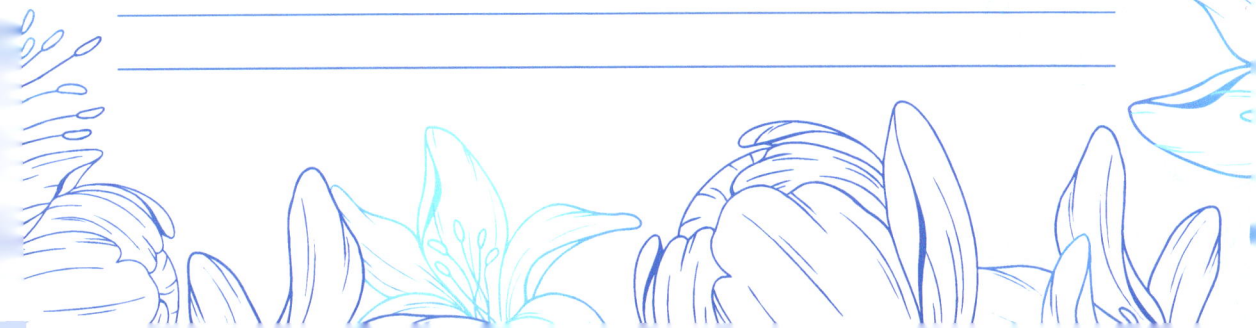

www.ingramcontent.com/pod-product-compliance
Lightning Source LLC
LaVergne TN
LVHW072057070426
835508LV00002B/142